# Cursive Handwriting Grades 2-6

## Children's Reading & Writing Education Books

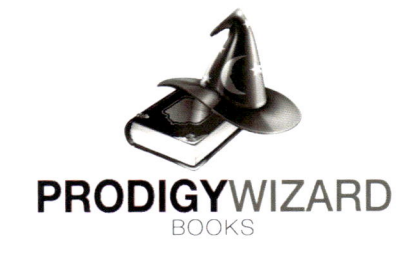

**PRODIGYWIZARD**
BOOKS

All Rights reserved. No part of this book may be reproduced or used in any way or form or by any means whether electronic or mechanical, this means that you cannot record or photocopy any material ideas or tips that are provided in this book

Copyright 2016

Trace the letters and words.

Rewrite them in the space provided.

Aa  Aa Aa Aa

Apple Apple Apple

Bb  Bb  Bb  Bb

Box  Box  Box  Box

Cc  Cc  Cc  Cc  Cc

Crab  Crab  Crab

Dd  Dd  Dd  Dd

Deer  Deer  Deer

Ee    Ee  Ee  Ee  Ee

Eagle  Eagle  Eagle

# Ff  Ff  Ff  Ff  Ff

## Fork  Fork  Fork

Gg  Gg  Gg  Gg

Gift  Gift  Gift

# Hh

Hh  Hh  Hh

Heart  Heart  Heart

*Ii    Ii  Ii  Ii  Ii*

*Igloo  Igloo  Igloo*

# Jj

## Juice

Kk  Kk  Kk  Kk

Kite  Kite  Kite  Kite

Ll   Ll Ll Ll

Leaf Leaf Leaf

*Mm Mm Mm*

*Monkey Monkey*

Nn  Nn Nn Nn

Note Note Note Note

Oo  Oo  Oo  Oo  Oo

Olive  Olive  Olive

*Pp*    *Pp Pp Pp*

*Pear Pear Pear Pear*

Qq  Qq  Qq  Qq

Question  Question

Rr    Rr  Rr  Rr

Rose  Rose  Rose

*Ss*     *Ss Ss Ss*

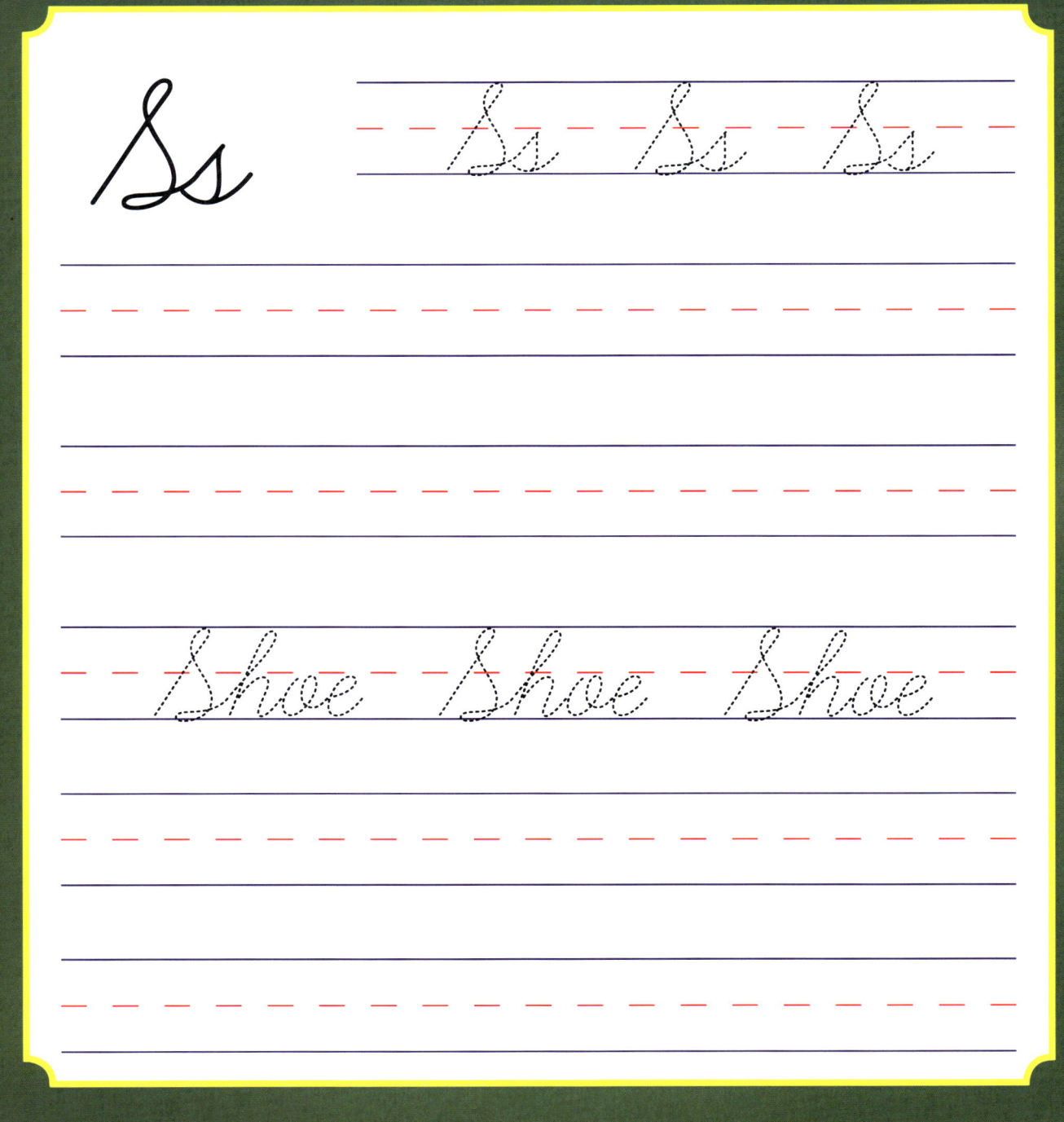

*Shoe Shoe Shoe*

# Tt

Tt Tt Tt Tt

Train Train Train

# Uu

*Uu Uu Uu*

*Umbrella Umbrella*

*Vv    Vv  Vv  Vv*

*Vase  Vase  Vase  Vase*

*Ww    Ww   Ww*

*Window   Window*

Xx  Xx  Xx  Xx

X-ray  X-ray

Yy Yy Yy Yy

Yacht Yacht Yacht

Zz Zz Zz Zz

Zoo Zoo Zoo Zoo

Trace the sentences and rewrite them in the space provided.

*I love to write.*

*Girls love dolls.*

*I like to have fun.*

This is my pet.

*This is my dress.*

*This balloon is red.*

The shoes are blue.

*Please close the door.*

The sky is blue.